God Bless Amei and Other Patriotic Piano Solos

Complements All Piano Methods

Table of Contents

God Bless America And Other Patriotic Piano Solos Level 5 is designed for use with the fifth book of any piano method.

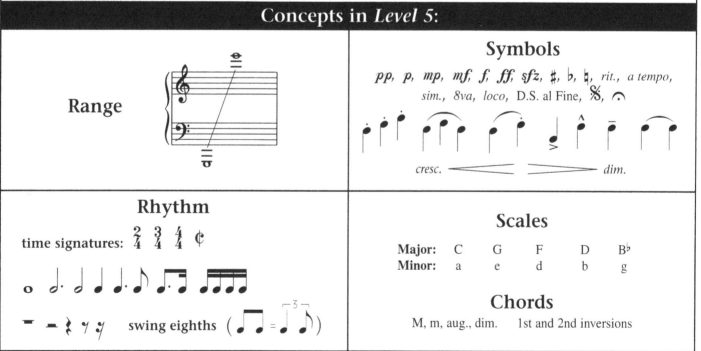

ISBN 978-0-634-04118-1

CORPORATION

7777 W. BLUEMOUND RD. P.O. BOX 13819 MILWAUKEE, WI 53213

Visit Hal Leonard Online at
www.halleonard.com

America, The Beautiful

Words by Katherine Lee Bates
Music by Samuel A. Ward
Arranged by Fred Kern

bove the fruit - ed plain! A - mer - i - ca! A -
dimmed by hu - man tears! A - mer - i - ca! A -

mer - i - ca! God shed His grace on thee, and
mer - i - ca! God mend thine ev - 'ry flaw, con -

crown thy good with broth - er - hood from sea to shin - ing
firm thy soul in self - con - trol, thy lib - er - ty in

sea. O law.

law.

cresc.

This Land Is Your Land

Words and Music by Woody Guthrie
Arranged by Fred Kern

Stars And Stripes Forever

By John Philip Sousa
Arranged by Mona Rejino

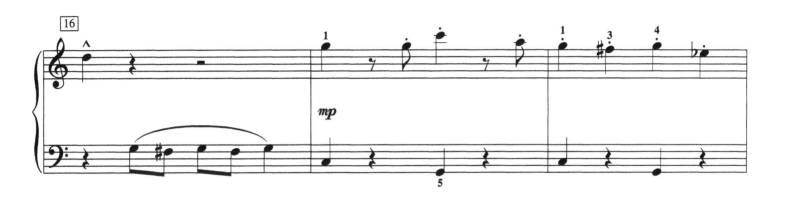

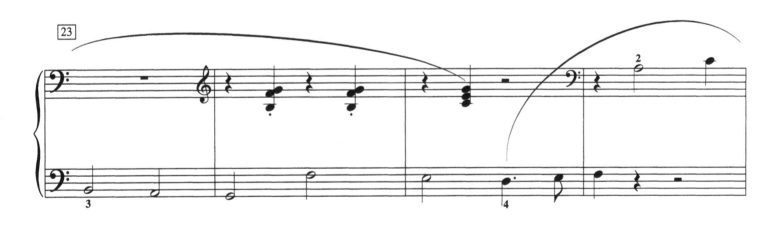

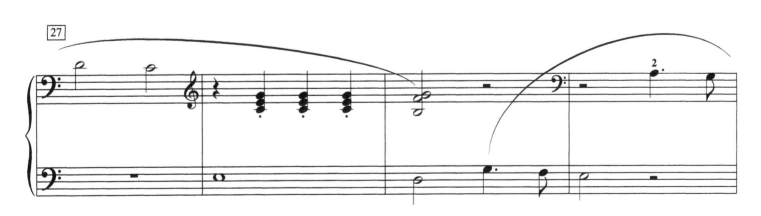

We Shall Overcome

Musical and Lyrical Adaptation by Zilphia Morton, Frank Hamilton,
Guy Carawan and Pete Seeger
Inspired by African American Gospel Singing, members of the Food and Tobacco Workers Union,
Charleston, SC, and the Southern Civil Rights Movement
Arranged by Mona Rejino

Moderately slow, with expression (♩ = 88)

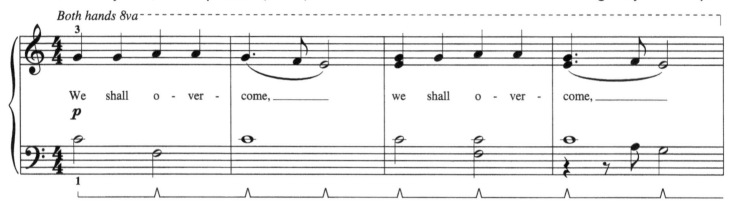

We shall o-ver-come, _____ we shall o-ver-come, _____

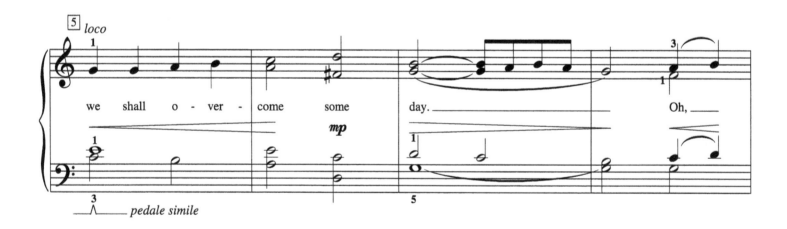

we shall o-ver-come some day. _____ Oh, _____

deep in my heart I do be-lieve we shall o-ver-

Battle Hymn Of The Republic

Words by Julia Ward Howe
Music by William Steffe
Arranged by Fred Kern

Stately March (♩ = 92)

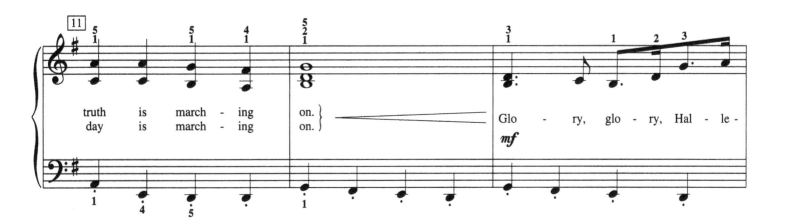

truth is march - ing on.
day is march - ing on.
Glo - ry, glo - ry, Hal - le -

mf

lu - jah! Glo - ry, glo - ry, Hal - le - lu - jah!

Glo - ry, glo - ry, Hal - le - lu - jah! His truth is march - ing

1.

on. *f* *rit.* *mp* I have

2.

Calmly

on. *a tempo*

rallentando

Much slower, expressive

pp In the beau - ty of the lil - ies, Christ was born a - cross the sea. With a

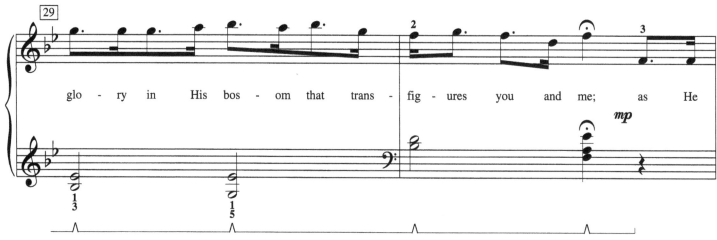

glo - ry in His bos - om that trans - fig - ures you and me; as He

mp

died to make men ho - ly let us die to make men free, while

cresc.

God is march - ing on. Glo - ry, glo - ry, Hal - le -
lu - jah! Glo - ry, glo - ry, Hal - le - lu - jah!
Glo - ry, glo - ry Hal - le - lu - jah! His truth is march - ing

Broadly

on.

Let There Be Peace On Earth

Words and Music by Sy Miller
and Jill Jackson
Arranged by Mona Rejino

To Coda ⊕

peace that was meant to be. _____ With
this be my sol - emn vow: _____ to

poco a poco cresc.

mf

God as our Fa - ther, _____

bro - thers all are we. _____

Let me walk with my broth - er _____ in

D.S. al Coda

per - fect har - mo - ny. _____

17

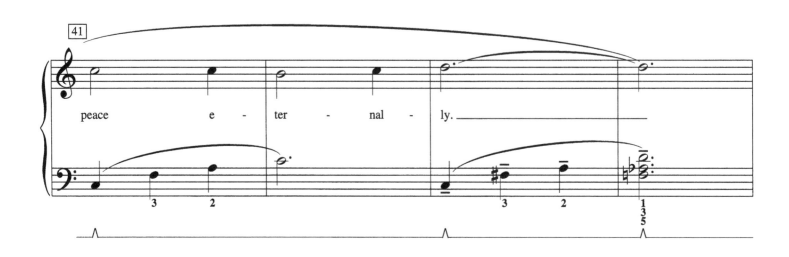

18

Pray For Our Nation

Words and Music by David T. Clydesdale
and Rick Logan
Arranged by Phillip Keveren

land. He calls us to be hum - ble, He

calls us now to pray. If we will seek His face and turn from

sin - ful ways, He prom - i - ses to hear us, He prom - i - ses to

guide us, He prom - i - ses for - give - ness and to heal our

land. It's time to pray, pray,

God Bless America

Words and Music by Irving Berlin
Arranged by Phillip Keveren

With majesty (♩ = 92)

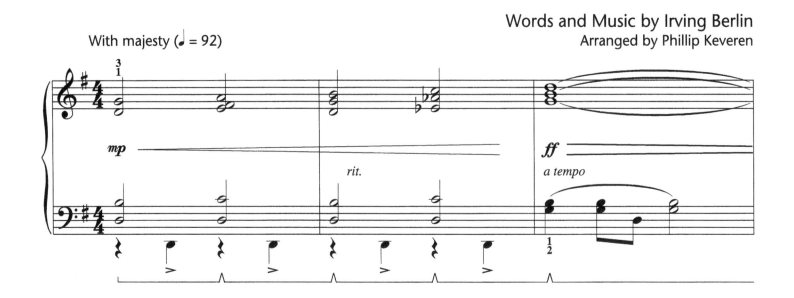

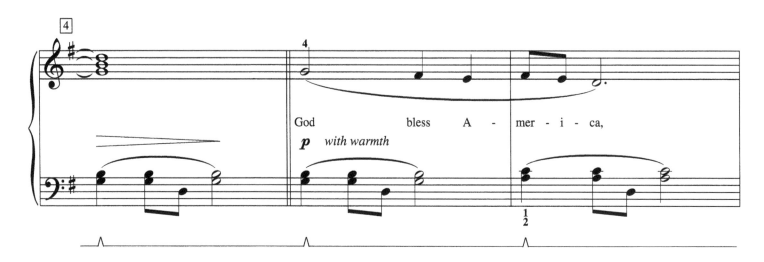

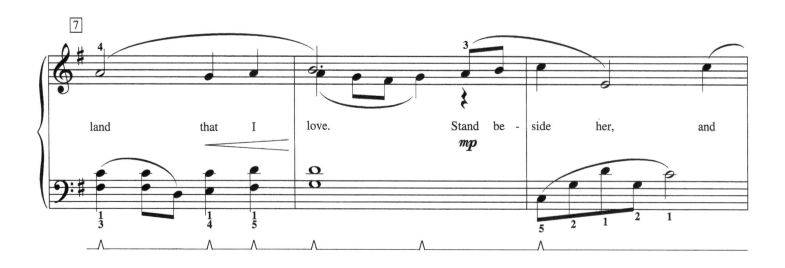

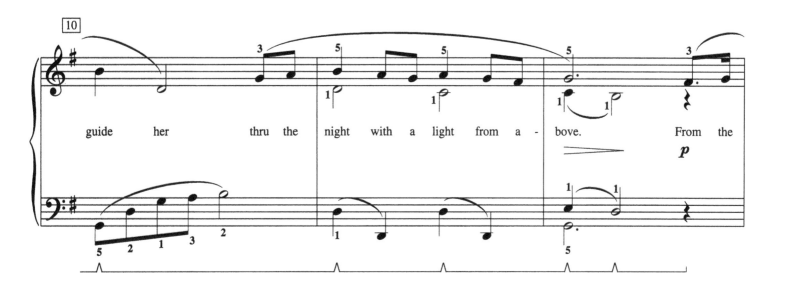

guide her thru the night with a light from a - bove. From the

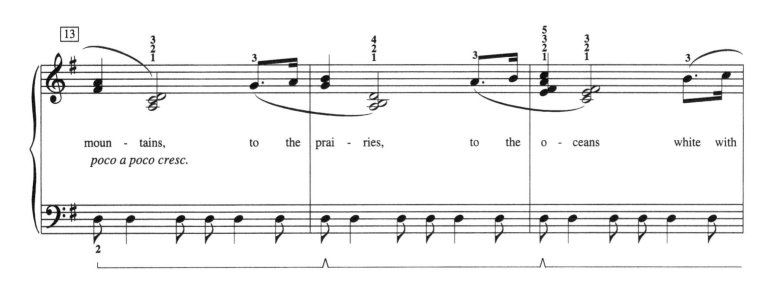

moun - tains, to the prai - ries, to the o - ceans white with

poco a poco cresc.

foam. God bless A - mer - i - ca, my

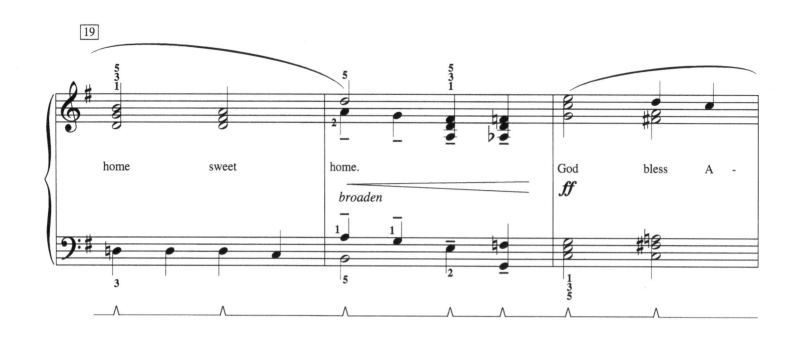

home   sweet   home.   God   bless   A -

broaden   **ff**

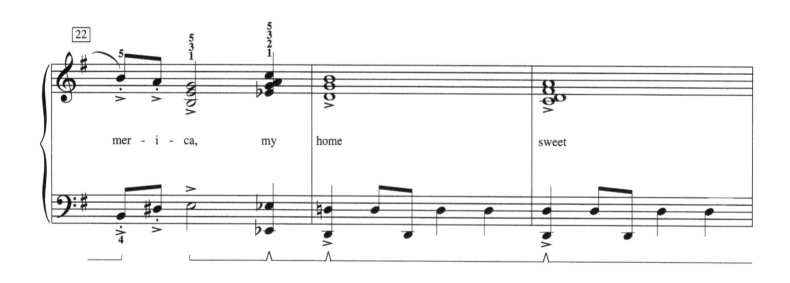

mer - i - ca,   my   home   sweet

home.   *molto rit.*   **sffz**